RHYTHM

A 28-DAY DEVOTIONAL ABOUT **GROWING CLOSER TO GOD**

for teenagers

INTRODUCTION

For a lot of us, music is a central part of our lives. In the car, at school, or even just walking through a store, music plays in the background. Music can be more than fun and entertainment for us, though. While the best rhythms and beats can make us want to dance or help us focus to handle our work, they also help us understand how we can develop healthy habits for our spiritual lives. With the right habits, we can set ourselves up to grow closer to God than we could ever imagine.

For the next four weeks, we'll take some time to explore how we can build rhythms that help us connect with God in new ways. We'll discover how to build a strong rhythm that can sustain us through whatever life brings our way. We'll look at how to create rhythms that help us **spend time with God**, **use our gifts**, **share our stories**, and **spend time with others**.

As we do, we'll consider...

- What happens when we view God as someone we can connect with instead of someone we get things from?
- What if God gave us everything we needed to start making a difference in our communities right now?
- What if we could help people understand who God is by being intentional with the things we say and do?
- What if we looked at friendships as more than a chance to hang out and have fun, but also as a chance to grow together in faith?

Let's find out.

HOW TO USE THIS BOOK

This devotional is meant to be read over 28 days, but don't worry too much about the days and numbers. If you miss a day, or a week, or even a whole month or two, that's okay! This book will be right here waiting for you when you're ready to come back. Just pick it up right where you left off.

But if you do use this book every day for the next 28 days, here's what you can expect…

- **BIG IDEAS:** At the start of every week, you'll get a **big idea** to consider all week long. These big ideas are short and easy-to-remember summaries of the ideas we're exploring. We'll focus on a new big idea each week.

- **DAILY DEVOTIONALS:** On most days, you'll read a short devotional and a short passage of Scripture. Then you'll be given five reflection questions and a daily challenge to help you turn what you've read into next steps.

- **WEEKLY REST DAYS:** Once a week, you'll be invited to take a break from your regular routine and spend time with God in a different way. Rather than reading a new passage of Scripture, you'll reflect on what you've already read as you discover another way to grow. Whether it's a prayer walk, a conversation with a friend, or an act of generosity, each of these experiences are designed to help you develop one of these four spiritual habits:

    o **Spending time with God** in a variety of ways.
    o **Spending time with others** who help you grow.
    o **Using your gifts** to love God and others.
    o **Sharing your story of faith** with others.

- **LOOKING BACK REFLECTIONS:** At the very end of this devotional, you'll be given a few more reflection questions to help you remember how God spoke to you, encouraged you, and challenged you over the last 28 days.

WEEK 1

Have you ever...

- Wanted to know how to build up your connection with God?
- Wondered how connecting with God could help you grow?
- Needed help understanding what spending time with God could look like?
- Wondered if there was one set way to connect with God?
- Felt like you just didn't have time in your schedule to read your Bible or pray?
- Struggled to make a consistent space to put your faith into practice?

If your faith feels like it could use a refresh, maybe rebuilding your rhythms could help it come alive.

Create rhythms to spend time with God.

DAY 1
Create rhythms to spend time with God.

Have you ever thought about what goes into making your favorite songs? At first, you might think about the rhythm, the lyrics, or how it makes you feel, but behind those things are hours and hours of practice. Putting together a hit song doesn't happen by accident, and making space in your life for the right habits can help you stay on the right track.

In today's reading, you'll follow the story of a woman who wanted to grow closer to Jesus. She wanted to be so close, she even came to dinner uninvited. While she was there, she took another step toward a connection with Jesus by pouring an expensive jar of perfume on his feet. She wasn't performing an over the top act for Jesus, but she wanted to build up a new type of relationship with him. With each step, Jesus met her and welcomed her.

When we start to build rhythms of connection, God will meet us right where we are. It doesn't matter what we've done or what we've been through. God will always meet us. We just have to remember to focus on the connection. Our rhythms should be spaces for new connection with God and not a performance, and don't need to look like anyone else's. God has made each of us uniquely and understands all of our lives are different. You could take a walk in nature, journal, or listen to a worship song. All that matters is that you **create rhythms to spend time with God**.

READ: *Luke 7:36-50*

DAY 2
Create rhythms to spend time with God.

Do you know what it's like to be dehydrated? Your mouth gets dry and you might end up tired or dizzy. When those feelings come over you, the only solution is to drink water and rest.

In today's reading, Jesus reminds us of the importance of having a good source of water. In the middle of the day, Jesus went to a well to get some water and met a woman there. After talking for a bit, he said to her *whoever drinks the water I give them will never thirst*. Could you imagine never being thirsty or dehydrated again? That would be incredible — but he wasn't talking about our physical thirst, but about what happens when we build strong rhythms of connection with God.

When we make a habit of spending time with God, we're constantly connected to the life God gives to us. It's like having a never ending source of water for our faith. By making these rhythms of connection, we can go to God for everything we need and then head back out into the world.

Making a habit of spending time with God does so much to prepare you for the road ahead. God's presence can restore us, give us wisdom, and provide hope for us to live our lives. It all starts with making space to meet with God and being open to what God will teach you. Our rhythms of spending time with God keep us connected to the good things God gives us.

READ: *John 4:13-14*

Has there ever been a time when your faith felt like
it was drying out? How did you respond?

How does this passage help you understand
what it means to connect with God?

How does spending time with God help us grow in our faith?

What's a small way you can connect with God this week?

What's one step you can take to build a stronger rhythm for connecting with God today?

Today, set aside a few minutes to pray and connect with God.

DAY 3

Create rhythms to spend time with God.

There are some things in life we tend to overcomplicate. We might spend hours analyzing something a friend said or interpret a simple text message in a hundred ways. It's hard to believe, but there are times when things can be as simple as they appear.

In today's reading, Jesus gives his followers a simple way to understand how to connect with him. He uses the image of a vine and branches so they can visualize exactly what it looks like to stay connected to God. If they want to grow and *bear fruit*, then they'll need to work on staying close to Jesus.

We might imagine spending time with God as a series of specific actions we have to perform on a regular basis, but that's just one part of it. Spending time with God can be as simple as clearing our heads and saying a prayer. It's all about making time in our lives to focus on our relationship with God.

When Jesus told his disciples he was the vine, it was to help them understand the importance of staying connected to his life and his teachings. Spending time with God takes intention and planning. It's not something that just happens on its own. It's an important part of growing in your faith and understanding of who God is. The more we connect with God, the faster and stronger our faith can grow. So remember to make space in your life to connect with God, even if it's by doing something simple.

READ: *John 15:1-5*

Who in your life best models spending time with God regularly? What could you learn from them?

What's something from this passage that was new to you?

How does staying close to God help us "bear fruit" in our lives?

What happens when we simplify the way we connect with God?

What's one simple way you can spend time with God today?

Today, place a repeating reminder in your phone to say a quick prayer and connect with God.

DAY 4

Create rhythms to spend time with God.

Go to church. Read the Bible. Pray. When we think about ways to spend time with God, these are often the things at the top of the list. While there are so many ways we can make space to connect with God, learning to pray regularly is one of the best places to start building your rhythm.

In today's reading, you'll see how Jesus taught his disciples to pray. He wanted to give them a clear model for what their own prayers could look like. So, he taught them how to pray for God's will, their daily needs, forgiveness, and protection. This model is actually a really simple way to begin building up your own prayer rhythm.

If you need help creating a rhythm of prayer, you can start by reciting these words each day or a few times a week. The great thing about prayer is it is so accessible. Whenever you feel like praying, you can simply stop what you're doing and say a few words of prayer to God. That's what makes prayer such a great starting point for building up a regular time for connection with God.

You can take a few moments to pray the words Jesus gave his disciples or talk with God in a different way. No matter what you choose to say, God is simply looking to make a connection with you to help you keep growing in your faith.

READ: *Matthew 6:5–14*

Before today, how did you understand prayer? What's new for you?

What's something from this passage that surprised you?

How can praying help us re-center and focus on God?

**How has prayer made a difference in your life
or the lives of people around you?**

What's one way you can creatively connect with God today?

Today, use Jesus' model to pray.

DAY 5

Create rhythms to spend time with God.

Do you ever wish you had a few more hours in your day? If you did, you might be able to squeeze in some extra homework or get a couple more hours of practice before your recital or game. For a lot of us, when we realize we're short on time, the ways we spend time with God can be pushed aside to make sure we get to other things first — but it doesn't have to be this way.

During one of Jesus' most famous teachings, he taught his disciples to seek out God's kingdom first. No matter what was happening in their lives, one of their top priorities was to focus on building their relationship with God. So how do we learn to focus on God even when we're busy?

The rhythms we set get to be completely unique to our lives and schedules. If you've got a lot of stuff happening in the early morning, you can spend time with God in the evening. If your only free time is on the weekend, then you can adjust your rhythms to spend time with God then. There's no one right way or time to connect with God, and you're free to adjust your rhythms as your schedule changes. What's most important is making space in your life to stay connected to what God is doing and teaching you. When life feels busy, you can still choose to seek God's kingdom first by building habits that work with your schedule.

READ: *Matthew 6:33*

Before today, how did you typically understand "quiet time?" Was it something that had to happen at a certain time in your day or week?

Why do you think Jesus would make connecting with God so simple and flexible for us?

How can focusing on seeking God change the way you approach your life and daily responsibilities?

What does it look like for you to seek God's kingdom first? Who could help you get started?

What's one way you can prioritize spending time with God's community today?

Today, think through your schedule for the next few days and plan a time to connect with God.

DAY 6

Create rhythms to spend time with God.

When a flashlight starts to run out of power, a few things can happen. The light might flash unexpectedly, or it may not shine as brightly. The same thing can happen to our faith when we aren't consistent in how we stay connected — or charged up — with God.

In today's reading, David writes a psalm about how deeply God knows him. Their relationship is so close because of all the time David spends with God. When we make time in our schedules and spend it with God, we grow closer — just like in any other relationship. When we're inconsistent in our habits, our connection with God might feel dry, or disconnected.

To keep your faith at its strongest and brightest, you'll need to develop a set rhythm for how you spend time with God. Whether it's through prayer, walks in nature, or reading your Bible, building up a consistent rhythm for connecting with God will help you in so many ways. If you do have a few moments of inconsistency, that's okay. You can give yourself grace and start rebuilding your rhythm the next day.

Choosing to spend time with God is the most important way to strengthen your faith and connection with God. So, how can you get started? If you haven't yet, start with a small connection and let it build over time. Do your best to stay consistent in your habits so your faith can shine bright in the world.

READ: *Psalm 139:1-6*

**What are the habits and routines you have right now?
How can you adapt those to include time with God?**

Why is building a steady rhythm important for growing our faith?

In what ways does this passage inspire you to grow?

Who can help keep you accountable as you build up a steady rhythm to connect with God?

What's one change you can make to help you build a rhythm?

Today, invite some friends to join you as you learn to connect with God consistently.

DAY 7

Today, take time to practice the spiritual habit of **spending time with God**.

This week, you've spent time learning about how to create rhythms to help you spend time with God. Today, take some time to disconnect from being online. Log out of your social media accounts or turn off your computer and spend time connecting with God in a new way.

Disconnect from being online to create new rhythms.

WEEK 2

Have you ever...

- Considered the difference you could make when you work with others?
- Wondered about the ways you could better understand your role in the world?
- Struggled to know or understand the gifts God has given you?
- Felt like you needed more experience or time before you could help others?
- Struggled to find a place where you fit in and could help?
- Felt like your gifts weren't as good as the ones you see in others?

If you've ever wanted to connect with your purpose, maybe recreating your rhythms could help you find your place.

Create rhythms to use your gifts.

DAY 8

Create rhythms to use your gifts.

There's something really incredible about live music. From the performers to the lights and sound, the whole crew is able to use their unique gifts and talents to make something amazing. It's so powerful to see all those years of experience and practice get poured into every part of the performance.

God has given each of us unique gifts and abilities. You'll read about some of these in today's reading. When we've got a rhythm to stay connected to God, we can start to understand our gifts and learn about how they can help us serve others. When we all learn to use our gifts well, it's like all of the parts of your favorite concert happening seamlessly.

So what do you think your gifts are? There are probably areas of your life that come naturally to you, like sports, games, or school. You might have a great singing voice or experience empathy towards others easily. Maybe you need to spend more time exploring your gifts and talents to see what God has given you.

No matter how you've been gifted, you can use those things to help support what God is doing in the world. Together, with other followers of Jesus, you can build up a rhythm of using your gifts to have a positive impact on your community. Whether it's your spiritual gifts, hobbies, skills, or character traits, God has given you a unique set of skills and abilities. Take time to learn what they are and how you can **create rhythms to use your gifts**.

READ: *Romans 12:6–8*

**Before today, what did you know about gifts
and what they are? What's new for you?**

**How does this passage help you understand the gifts you've
been given and the role you play in your community?**

**How does building a connection with God help us
understand our gifts and how to use them?**

How can you encourage others as they learn to use their own gifts?

What's one way you can use a gift to help someone today?

Today, make a list of the gifts God has given you and think through ways you might be able to use these to help others.

DAY 9

Create rhythms to use your gifts.

When we think about people with gifts, we tend to think of actors, athletes, and musicians. We might even think about a few people at our school who are on the path to earn a scholarship for what they do. It's rare for us to think of *ourselves* as gifted, but that's not what the Bible tells us.

Today's reading talks about some of the ways God gifts people. It's important to not just see the gifts themselves, but the reasons *for* those gifts. God equips people so that *the body of Christ may be built up*. God gives specific skills to specific people so that Christians all around the world can have their faith strengthened and be encouraged as they grow.

You've been given skills, talents, and abilities that are unique to you. With these gifts, you get to have a special impact on the world. When Christians all around the world use their gifts together, they help everyone take a step toward knowing Jesus.

No matter how long you've been following Jesus, God has a unique space in the world for you, and your talents and abilities can help make a difference in the lives of people around you. Whether it's through a form of leadership, unique insight into your community, or the ability to organize events, God can use you. When we make rhythms to use our gifts, we can connect with our purpose and help point others to Jesus. Using your gifts truly can help make a difference.

READ: *Ephesians 4:11-14*

**What are some ways you've see people use their gifts
to make a difference in their communities?**

How can using our gifts help us point others to Jesus?

How can you work together with other Christians to use your gifts?

What are some gifts or talents you haven't explored or developed just yet?

What's one way you can use one of your gifts today?

Today, ask someone about
the gifts they have.

DAY 10

Create rhythms to use your gifts.

Discovering your gifts can feel like solving a puzzle. There are some pieces that line up right away and are easy to figure out. Then, there are others that take a little more time and patience to put together. Thankfully, no matter how long it takes us to discover our gifts, God has a plan to use them.

In today's reading, you see one of the places where Paul talks about the way God gives us gifts. He says there are different kinds of gifts, but God works through each one of them. He even says there are *different kinds of service*, but all of it points to the same God. So when it's time for us to start thinking about which gifts God has given us, we have the freedom to explore.

Whether or not you have a general idea of the ways you are gifted, you can start trying new things to discover what sticks with you. You can try taking on new responsibilities with your family or your youth group. You can decide to try out for the things that interest you. You have the freedom to try new things and see what works best for you. Exploring isn't your only option — you can ask others about their perspective of you. Your family, church leaders, and friends might have some helpful insight into the ways you're gifted. With the things you discover and guidance from your friends and family, you'll have a good idea of which gifts God has given you.

READ: *1 Corinthians 12:4–6*

How do you typically learn about your gifts, talents, or skills?

In what ways does using your gifts help
you grow and connect with God?

Why do you think God created so many different kinds of gifts?

How can you use some of your gifts to serve others today?

What's one way you can try to discover a new gift or skill today?

*Today, ask someone about
the gifts they see in you.*

DAY 11

Create rhythms to use your gifts.

Don't wait.

You might think you need time to really perfect your gifts. Maybe you've just discovered something new and you're thinking you've got to really master it before God can use it. That couldn't be any further from the truth.

In today's Scripture, you'll read a snippet of a letter from one of Jesus' closest followers. In it, he tells people to *use whatever gift you have received to serve others*. He doesn't tell them to wait until their voices stop cracking or until they've learned the best leadership skills. Peter understands God will use our gifts no matter what they look like. We just have to show up and trust God.

If you've got a gift that's exciting you right now, use it. Talk about it. Work with your youth pastor or youth leaders to figure out how to harness all of your passion and energy as soon as possible. With some creativity, you can come up with a plan to help you get connected and start a new rhythm for using those gifts. It may not be perfect at first, but every step of faith is a chance to learn something new and grow in your faith. If it does start off rocky, know God sees your heart and how you're trying to serve others.

Don't wait until you've perfected the gifts you've been given. Take a chance to try something new and trust God to use you and your gifts right now.

READ: *1 Peter 4:10*

**Why do you think we often wait until we've perfected
our skills and gifts before we use them?**

**How can using our gifts right now help us grow
our relationships with God and with others?**

**In what ways does this passage inspire
you to learn about your gifts?**

How can you overcome the fears you may have about using gifts?

Who could you encourage to use their gifts today?

*Today, use your gifts to
help serve someone.*

DAY 12

Create rhythms to use your gifts.

Even when we have a good idea of our gifts, we might not always have a place to use them. You might realize you're great at throwing Christmas parties, but it's the middle of July and a bit early to be thinking about the holidays. Even though you may not have the best place to use your gift *right now*, there are still some things you *can* do.

In today's reading, you'll hear about the Spirit of *power, love and self-discipline* that God gives to everyone who follows Jesus. When we don't know exactly how to use our gifts, *discipline* is an important word. As we're waiting to figure out the role our gifts can play, we can keep working on developing our skills and abilities. We can continue to practice, learn, and harness our gifts so we're even more competent and skilled.

While we're making rhythms of discipline and practice, we can also work with others to think about new ways to use our gifts. Together, you might imagine a new scenario or an interesting event for your youth group where your gifts could fit perfectly. You might even realize the perfect place for your gifts was in front of you all along. If you still can't think of anything, that might be a sign to work on developing some other gifts while you're waiting for the right opportunity. As you do, trust God and know that if you've been given a gift, you'll have the chance to use it.

READ: *2 Timothy 1:6-7*

Have you ever felt like you had a gift, but couldn't find a way to use it? How did you respond to those feelings?

How can discipline help us grow in our faith and the ways we use our gifts?

What's something from this passage that surprised you?

**How can we encourage others while they discover
new ways to use their own gifts?**

How can learn something new about your gifts today?

*Today, brainstorm with friends some
creative ways you could use all your gifts.*

DAY 13

Create rhythms to use your gifts.

Have you ever looked at the way someone has been gifted and deep down you thought, "I wish I could do that." When we look at the talents and abilities of others, we might start to compare ourselves and become discouraged about our own gifts. If you've ever feel that way, just remember the purpose behind your gifts — to help the people around you see Jesus in a new way.

Today's reading comes from one of Jesus' most famous teachings. In it, he told his disciples they were *the salt of the earth* and *the light of the world*. That means each of them had a unique purpose and could make a difference in the lives of the people around them. The same goes for you, too. Instead of comparing gifts or abilities, you can remind yourself that God has you in the exact right place to make a difference in your community.

We all have different gifts and some are more developed than others, but that doesn't mean your gifts are more or less important than someone else's. Instead, we can *work together* to use our gifts to focus on showing the world who Jesus is. We can even celebrate each other for the ways God has gifted us. When we see others using their gifts, we can resist comparing ourselves by instead trusting God has us exactly where we are for a reason. We all have a chance to use our gifts to serve others.

READ: *Matthew 5:13–16*

Has there been a time when you felt discouraged about the way
God gifted you? How did you work through those feelings?

How can you build your trust in God for the
times you may feel discouraged?

What can you do to remind yourself of the unique
role God created for you in the world?

Who could you talk to about using your gifts in the world?

What's one way you can celebrate the way
your friends have been gifted?

Today, offer a specific compliment to
a friend about one of their gifts.

DAY 14

Today, take time to practice the spiritual habit of **using your gifts** to serve God and others.

For the last few days, you've been exploring what can happen when we make rhythms to use our gifts. Today, use your gifts to serve someone you know. Whether it's a teacher, your pastor, or a stranger, be creative and think through a way your gifts can help them.

Serve someone you know.

WEEK 3

Have you ever...

- Felt inspired by a story someone shared with you?
- Wondered if you had a story to share with others?
- Struggled with wanting to share your story but didn't want to overstep or make people feel uncomfortable?
- Felt like each time you talked about your faith, it came across awkward or forced?
- Questioned whether your story and experiences were even compelling?
- Wondered how to get started talking with others about your faith?

If sharing your story seems uncomfortable to you, maybe rebuilding your rhythm could help change your perspective.

Create rhythms to share your story.

DAY 15

Create rhythms to share your story.

As humans, we crave stories we connect with on a deep level. So it shouldn't surprise us that many of the songs that mean so much to us have compelling stories. Whether it's the lyrics themselves or the story behind how a song was made, we can become so interested in it, we want to share it with whoever will listen.

In the book of Acts, Philip meets someone from out of town and it changes his life forever. When this traveler had questions, Philip took time to share about his personal experiences with Jesus. When he shared his story, he inspired this man to follow Jesus himself.

Just like Philip, you have a story about how God has been working in your life. Those stories, with Jesus at the center, have the potential to change the lives of the people around us. Sharing your story can feel a little scary and daunting, but taking the risk to share such a personal thing can be so rewarding. You don't need to be the best speaker or nail the delivery. Instead, God invites you to create rhythms that help you communicate your experiences authentically.

Whether it's through music, art, or a conversation with someone, telling your story can inspire others and draw them closer to God. So, don't be afraid to step out in faith and share your story with those around you. **Create rhythms to you share your story** and let the light of Jesus shine through.

READ: *Acts 8:26-40*

Why do you think stories can have such an impact on us?

**How can our own stories help inspire people
and help them connect with God?**

How can sharing your story help you grown in your faith?

What would it look like for you to create a rhythm of sharing your story?

Who is one person you could share part of your story with today?

Today, reflect on your life and journal about some of the important moments in your story.

DAY 16

Create rhythms to share your story.

Have you ever been asked to share your faith story? Maybe you've felt like you don't have one, or you're not sure how to put it into words. No matter how long we've been following Jesus, we all have a story worth sharing.

In today's passage, we read about a woman who met Jesus at a well. After talking with him, she ran back to her village and told everyone about him. This woman didn't have all the answers or a perfect faith, but she wanted to share her experience with others — and it changed their lives.

Your faith story doesn't have to be perfect. Maybe you grew up going to church, or maybe you found God in a moment of crisis. You might be still figuring things out, but sharing your journey can show others that they're not alone and that there's hope in Jesus.

So, how do you start to figure out your story? You can begin by reflecting on what God has done in your life. You can think through the ways you've changed since you've been following Jesus. It might be easiest to think about how you've been experiencing Jesus show up in your life lately. If you need help, don't be afraid to ask. Your youth leaders and youth pastor would love to help you understand your story and learn how to share it. Because when we make rhythms to share our story, we can help others experience Jesus.

READ: *Galatians 2:20*

Describe a time when you shared your story with someone else. What did you learn? How did it impact you?

What are some of the things God has done in your life that you could share?

How can your habits for connecting with God help you share your story?

What are the barriers keeping you from sharing your story? How can you work through these?

What's one step you could take to be more comfortable sharing your story?

Today, ask someone to share a part of their story with you.

DAY 17

Create rhythms to share your story.

Have you ever wanted to share your faith story with someone, but were worried about making them feel uncomfortable? It's totally normal to feel like that, and there are ways to share your story without pushing others away or making them uncomfortable.

In today's reading, we'll see how Jesus told his disciples not to worry about what to say when they are about to share their stories. He told them everything they'd need to know would come from the Holy Spirit. If we go into a conversation about our faith with the goal of converting someone, we might accidentally make someone feel trapped. Instead, we can focus on sharing our personal experiences with God, and create space for a good conversation.

One way we can help others become more comfortable is to listen first. You can ask questions and show interest in *their* story before sharing your own. This shows you care about them and you're not just trying to push your own beliefs on them. When you share your story, you can give them space to respond however they feel. It would be awesome if they chose to follow Jesus, but they also might have some follow up questions or want to talk about something else entirely.

We can learn to share our stories in ways that make people *more* comfortable. By listening first, sharing our experiences, and giving space for response, we can show our care for others while faithfully sharing our stories.

READ: *Luke 12:11–12*

Describe a time when someone shared their story with you. What did you learn? What was it like to listen to someone share?

Why do you think Jesus would teach his followers to put so much trust in the Holy Spirit?

How do you learn to connect with the Holy Spirit?

What are some ways you can be intentional about listening to others in your conversations?

What's one way you can create space for conversation when you share your story?

Today, thank God for guiding you as you learn to share your story.

DAY 18

Create rhythms to share your story.

Have you ever tried to share your faith story with someone, but it just didn't feel right? Maybe it felt forced or awkward, and you weren't sure what to do about it. Don't worry, you're not alone. Sharing your faith story can be tough, but it's important to remember that the outcome isn't entirely up to you.

Today's reading is about Jesus' parable of the sower. In this story, he describes a farmer who scattered seed on different types of soil. Some of the seed fell on rocky ground and didn't grow, while other seed fell on fertile soil and produced a pretty large harvest. Jesus told this story to help us see how we can plant the seeds of faith, but it's up to God to make them grow.

If sharing your faith story feels forced, it can help to remember that it's not your job to force someone to believe. Your job is to share your story in a genuine way and trust God with what comes next. It also might help to think about timing, too. Seeds needs the right conditions to grow, and sharing your story may need the right moment, too.

Even if things feel a bit awkward right now, that doesn't change the importance of your story. You never know how your words may impact someone down the road. So, keep sharing your story in a way that feels genuine to you, and trust that God is working behind the scenes.

READ: *Luke 8:5–15*

Has there been a time when sharing your story felt awkward? How did you respond? Who did you ask for help?

What does it look like to trust God with what happens after we share our stories?

What's something from this passage that stuck with you?

What does it look like for you to be genuine or authentic in how you share your story?

What's one change you can make to open yourself to trust God more?

Today, ask a friend to help you practice sharing your story.

DAY 19

Create rhythms to share your story.

Do you ever find yourself comparing your story with someone else's? If you've been in church any amount of time, you've probably heard a lot of different stories of faith. Whether they were about a dramatic moment in someone's life or about the powerful way God showed up for someone else, we may end up looking at our own stories as if they're small or not worth telling. But, God reminds us that each of our stories is as powerful as we let it be.

Today you'll read about a time when Paul talks about treasure in clay jars. His words were meant to encourage and remind people that though they might *feel* small, weak, or insignificant, God has placed something so powerful and beautiful inside *each* of us.

Your story doesn't need to be filled with dramatic moments or major life changes to be worth telling. In fact, some of those smaller, more everyday experiences can have a huge impact on others. Every small moment adds up to make a difference in someone's life.

What might seem like an ordinary story to you, is an extraordinary story in God's eyes. God has given you a unique experience and perspective of the world. Those experiences have the power to inspire and encourage others in ways that no one else can. So, rather than compare your story, embrace it. Trust God to use your story to make a difference in the people you choose to share it with. Love your story that is uniquely you.

READ: *2 Corinthians 4:7-9*

What do you think makes a good faith story?

What's something from this passage that stuck with you?

How can you trust God with your story?

**What types of everyday experiences could
make a difference on others?**

What's one way you can embrace your story today?

Today, talk with a friend and something
you're learning about your story.

DAY 20

Create rhythms to share your story.

Remember when Jesus met that woman at the well? She went into town and told everyone about her encounter with Jesus. She didn't wait until she had the right education or training. She just started talking with her community about what she saw, heard, and how she was going to live differently. Now, you get to follow in her footsteps.

Sharing your story can seem really scary. It's personal and there are probably more than a few bumps in our presentation. Yet, when we've experienced something as incredible as the love and life of Jesus, pushing through those feelings is absolutely worth it.

One place you can start sharing your story is through your words. In your conversations with others, you can tell them about the wisdom and guidance you've been getting from God. You can tell them about how God has been showing up in your life.

You can also share your story with your actions. The things you do communicate so much about who you are. People will learn your story from how you care for, serve, and protect others. Your actions are a reflection of your faith, and they can help others see what following God is like.

When it comes to sharing your story, you don't have to have it all figured you. God wants you to show up authentically and to let your words and actions reflect the ways Jesus is changing you. As you do, you can trust God to take care of whatever comes next.

READ: *John 4:28-29*

What questions do you still have about sharing your story?

From today's reading, how does the woman's response
inspire you to share your stories and experiences?

How have you seen God work through your
words and actions to impact others?

How do you know when it's the right time to share you story through words or through action?

What's one way you can share your story through action today?

Today, share your story with your family by serving them in a simple way.

DAY 21

Today, take time to practice the spiritual habit of **sharing your story of faith** with others.

This week has been all about creating rhythms to share your story. Today, take a step to share the ways you've been seeing God work in your life. Take the time to share a part of your story on social media.

Share part of your story on social media.

WEEK 4

Have you ever...

- Wondered how to make friends and new connections?
- Felt like you were better off doing things by yourself?
- Struggled to see how connecting with others could help you grow in your faith?
- Had a hard time connecting with other Christians?
- Wanted to know where you could go to find wisdom for your life?
- Wondered if there was anything you had to share?

If you've ever wanted to know the importance of community, maybe rebuilding your rhythm could give you a glimpse of what's possible in your relationships.

Create rhythms to spend time with others.

DAY 22

Create rhythms to spend time with others.

Our friends are really important people in our lives. They're the ones we laugh with and share our favorite moments with. But have you ever thought about *how* these people became your friends? Most likely, your friendships exist because you've spent a lot of time together.

In today's reading, we'll see what happens when the Early Church started spending more time together. As they made a habit out of connecting with each other, they started sharing meals together. Then, they started sharing what they owned and growing in their connection with God. Eventually, they were spending *every day* together hanging out and building up their relationship. It all started because they committed to following Jesus.

When we're committed to a goal or an idea, it's a lot easier to spend time together. That's why teams, squads, and casts can grow so close together. For us, we can choose to spend time with people who commit to knowing more about God's words, serving others, and praising God. When we center our friendships around these areas, we can grow like the Early Church did because we're investing in each other, our faith, and our community. From here, we can ask questions about each other's lives and learn about each other. We can have fun in our friendships as we serve God and our communities. And, who knows, you might end up having a new friend for life. But it all starts with choosing to **create rhythms to spend time with others**.

READ: *Acts 2:42-47*

Think through your friendships. How did you
meet your friends? What made you close?

What's something from this passage that inspires
you to approach your friendships differently?

How can being intentional with our friends
help us grow in our faith?

What are some of the challenges you've faced in building deeper friendships? How do you plan to work through these?

What's one step you can take to invest in your friendships today?

Today, thank your friends for sticking with you.

DAY 23

Create rhythms to spend time with others.

Maybe you feel like it'd be easier to take care of things on your own, or you're just really not that comfortable opening up to people. If this is the case, you might be tempted to brush off some friendships. While we live in a world that often tells us to focus on ourselves and our own success, God's community is focused on relationships and supporting others.

You might be familiar with the idea that we're all part of the body of Christ and each of us has a unique role to play. Just like the parts of a body work together to function properly, we can choose to work together as a community to live out our faith in the world.

When we spend time with others, we make time to learn from their experiences and understand our faith in new ways. We can pray for each other, give support during difficult times, and celebrate our victories. Community also helps us grow in our faith. We can encourage each other to take risks outside of our comfort zones, and hold each other accountable as we become more like Jesus.

Spending time with others helps us to see the bigger picture of what God is doing in the world. We can begin to understand the lives of others and how God is working within them. When we follow Jesus, we're choosing to let go of the idea of doing things alone. Instead, we're called to open up and embrace the power and love of a whole community.

READ: *1 Corinthians 12:27*

How do you see different gifts and skill
sets show up in your friendships?

How has being a part of a community impacted
your relationship with God?

Why do you think God designed us to be
a part of active communities?

**Why are we often tempted to try to do things on
our own? How can we work through this?**

**What's one change you can make to be more
focused on community and relationships?**

*Today, look for a simple way to
serve your faith community.*

DAY 24

Create rhythms to spend time with others.

Have you ever met someone who loved your favorite band or artist? There are some things that can give us an instant connection or a strong foundation to build a friendship, but finding people who share similar values and beliefs might be *more* difficult than finding someone who loves the same bands we do. So how do we find the right people and start forming healthy friendships?

Today's reading talks about honoring others over ourselves. This can be a helpful mindset as we start to think about how to build up our godly relationships. You can start by thinking about the types of things you honor and hold close. Doing this can help you start to filter through the types of core values and characteristics you might want in a friend.

While you're working on that list, you can find common spaces to get connected with people. Your youth group is a great example. There are teenagers just like who are trying to find other friends focused on Jesus. It might be a good idea to make time to be at events and other activities, too.

No matter how you get started, creating godly friendships takes time and effort. Sometimes things might click right away, but you'll still need a regular rhythm for spending time together. As you make connections, be patient, intentional, and loving. Trust God to provide the right friends at the right time as you keep growing in your faith. You can create friendships that honor God and others.

READ: *Romans 12:10*

Give an example of a time you met someone and things clicked right away. How did you keep investing in that friendship?

What does it look like to honor our friends above ourselves?

What's the importance of connecting with friends who have similar values and goals?

How can you develop a diverse community of friends?

What's one way you can honor your friends today?

*Today, organize a hang out
with your friends.*

DAY 25

Create rhythms to spend time with others.

Do you ever wonder if you *need* to hang out with other Christians? Maybe your beliefs don't exactly line up. Maybe you've struggled to feel like you fit in or belong. Those feelings are really common, but you can't just go through life alone. Having other Christians in your life is more important than we might realize.

Today's reading talks about making the choice to not give up *meeting together* and *encouraging one another*. When we choose to follow Jesus, we're also choosing to be part of a community of other people. We're joining into this incredible mosaic of cultures, beliefs, and opinions while we all learn how to become more like Jesus.

So while we might want to take a step back from people and focus on ourselves, we have to remember our faith was meant to be lived out and practiced with others. When we spend time with other Christians, we can share our struggles and the ways we see God moving through us.

If you find yourself struggling to connect with other Christians, don't give up just yet. Keep pursuing godly relationships and be open to trying new things. This might be a great chance to talk with your youth pastor and leaders about how you've been struggling. Together, you might dream up a few ideas to help other teenagers with similar feelings build godly relationships. So remember, even when you feel like you want to step back from other Christians, God invites you to connect with community.

READ: *Hebrews 10:24–25*

Describe a time when a friend helped you overcome a challenge. What was it like? In what ways did you grow closer?

Why do you think God invites us to encourage our friends in their faith journey?

How can your spiritual growth help influence the growth of your friends?

What do you think is the biggest challenge for encouraging others? How can you work through this?

What's one way you could help someone feel included in community?

Today, encourage a friend.

DAY 26

Create rhythms to spend time with others.

Where do you go when you need answers? From family and teachers to online forums, there are so many places we can go to find what we're looking for. When it comes to wisdom, so much of what we can learn comes from people who are older and more experienced than we are.

In today's reading, we'll see the importance of walking alongside of people who have more life experience. The author writes that those who *walk with the wise* can *become wise*. In our faith, we'll need people who have been walking with God longer than we have to help show us how to apply the things God has been teaching us.

If you want to get started learning from older Christians, the first step is to figure out who you could learn from. These are people who have been following Jesus longer than you, like older church people, family members, or even your youth leaders. From there, you can ask them to share how they became a Christian and what they've been learning lately. If there's something specific you need help with, you can ask if they have any experience with what you're going through.

Learning to seek wisdom from others is a valuable part of growing in your faith. As you ask others to share their stories and insight, you grow in your understanding of who God is. So, take a step of faith and spend time learning from others. You'll be surprised by what you learn.

READ: *Proverbs 13:20*

What wisdom have you learned from the older,
more experienced people in your life?

How can learning from older Christians help
us grow in our faith and relationships?

Why do you think wisdom is important for our lives?

What are some specific questions you could ask someone who's been following Jesus longer than you have?

What's one way you can regularly learn from older people in your church?

Today, ask your youth pastor or youth leader for ways to seek wisdom.

DAY 27

Create rhythms to spend time with others.

Older Christians aren't the only ones who can share what they've learned. You have things to share, too. You may not feel that way, but you have plenty of experiences and knowledge stored up. So what would it look like for you to share some of those things?

In today's reading, you'll hear from Peter, a leader of one of the earliest churches. He wrote to other leaders and reminded them to take care of the people in their communities. Peter invited them to share their wisdom and experiences to help younger Christians grow in their faith.

You're invited to do something similar. You can share the things you've learned about following Jesus with the next generation of people. Whether it's by serving in your kids' ministry at church, or choosing to be a good model for a younger sibling, there are all sorts of ways you can share the things you've learned. So much of how you can share your wisdom can even be done through your actions and the ways you treat others.

Regardless of how you share, God has filled you with all sorts of wisdom — even as you're still growing in your faith. It might be intimidating to share what you've learned, but it's a chance to practice our faith in a new way. Even in moments of uncertainty, when you start to share what you've learned with others, God will be with you every step of the way.

READ: *1 Peter 5:2–3*

What questions do you still have about spending time with others?

What's something from this passage that stood out to you?

How can passing on the wisdom and experiences you have help make a difference for someone else?

What advice would you give to someone younger than you?

**Who is one younger person you know that
you could share your wisdom with?**

*Today, connect with some friends
and come up with ways you could
pass on your wisdom to others.*

DAY 28

Today, take time to practice the spiritual habit of **spending time with others** in godly community.

For the last few days, you've been discovering what can happen when you make rhythms to spend time with others. Today, invite a friend or two to hang out or schedule a time to hang out in the future. Spend time watching a movie, going shopping, or doing something fun.

Make plans to spend time with a friend.

LOOKING BACK

So? How did it go?

For the last four weeks you've been exploring ways to build new rhythms or improve the ones you have. You've looked at the ways building a strong rhythm can have a huge impact on your relationships with God and with the people around you. So how have you grown?

What rhythms are you building to **spend time with God**? How have you been making time in your schedule to pray or be with God? How have you felt God shaping your heart? What are some new ways you've tried to connect with God? How do you want to keep growing?

What about the rhythms you've created to **use your gifts**? How have you been using the skills and resources God has given you? What's been fun about helping others? What's been challenging for you? What new skills have you been developing or practicing?

What about your rhythms for **sharing your story**? Who have you been sharing your faith with? How have you been prioritizing listening over speaking? What's been stretching for you? How have you seen your trust in God grow?

And what about your rhythms to **spend time with others**? Who have you been spending time with? How have you been including others in your time? How are you growing in your connection with God together?

Take a few minutes today to reflect back on the last 28 days. Write down some of the things you've been thinking about, processing, learning, or wondering.

What did you learn about yourself over the last 28 days?

What was the most challenging part of this book?

How can you continue to develop your spiritual habits?

What is one goal that you would like to accomplish in the next month?

What questions do you still have?

Today, find a space for yourself, turn on some music, and dance.

Made in United States
Troutdale, OR
11/30/2024

25534131R00070